Your Politics or Jesus

by L. C. Brown Bush

Copyright 2021: L. C. Brown Bush
All rights reserved.

While every precaution has been taken in the preparation of this book, the publisher assumes no responsibility for errors or omissions, or for damages resulting from the use of the information contained herein.

Dedications

*To my daughter and granddaughters
who encourage me to preach and laugh,
and be all that the Lord created me to be.*

Your Politics or Jesus
Table of Content

Chapter One
Why Are You Afraid?...*3*

Chapter Two
Repent and Believe *14*

Chapter Three
The Gatekeepers of Truth *25*

Chapter Four
Strong Delusion *38*

Chapter Five
A City or A Nation... *53*

Chapter Six
The Religious Political Strategy......................... *69*

Chapter Seven
The Seat of the Scornful *85*

Chapter Eight
Don't Be Conformed... *98*

Conclusion
 Call to Prayer...*109*

Politics

a. *Activity*[1] of government

b. *Activity* concerned with influencing government policy.

c. *Activity* concerned with the control of the government.

---

[1] The Art and Science

L. C. BROWN BUSH

Chapter One

Why Are You Afraid?

Seek peace and well-being for the city where I have sent you... and pray to the LORD on its behalf; for in its peace (well-being) you will have peace.'

For I know the plans and thoughts that I have for you,' says the LORD, 'plans for peace and well-being and not for disaster, to give you a future and a hope.

(Jeremiah 29:7 & 11 AMP)

JEREMIAH 29:11 is a favorite verse for many Christians. We buy wall hangings with that verse on it. It is the screen saver on our computer. And by it, we encourage ourselves and our children to believe we have a bright future guaranteed by the

Lord. We apply that promise individually, but actually, it is a *collective promise* given to the people of God at a time when they felt abandoned by the Lord and fearful about their future. Jeremiah 29:11 were words of *comfort and security* that God spoke to his people who were living as captives in a pagan nation. They were surrounded by people that did not think or worship like them, and they were afraid. And yet God sends a message to them by the prophet Jeremiah promising them security and a bright future... *but it was a promise that came with conditions.*

*"Build houses and **settle down.**"*

(Jeremiah 29:5)

Settle down... if the people of God wanted to embrace the future and hope that God was promising them, they would need to settle down, adjust to their new environment, then work and pray for the peace of that pagan nation. In the peace of that pagan nation, *God promised* that his people would have peace. In the prosperity and well-being of that nation, *God promised* that his people would enjoy prosperity and hope for the future. Moreover, almost a thousand years later, the Lord gave a similar directive and promise to early Christians living in a *Roman dominated* world.

> *First of all, then, **I urge** that petitions (specific requests), prayers, intercessions (prayers for others) and thanksgivings be offered on behalf of **all people**, for kings and all who are in [positions of] high authority, **so that we may live a peaceful and quiet life** in all godliness and dignity.*
> *(I Timothy 2:2-1 AMP)*

"You of little faith. Why are you afraid?[2]" That is what Jesus asked his disciples when the storm was

---

[2] Matthew 8:26

raging, and their boat was filling up with water. *Why are you afraid when I am in the boat with you?* The Lord asked the question, but really, he knew the answer. His disciples thought the problem was too big for him. They thought the raging storm was about to overpower them and Jesus. And they wanted to know how the Lord could be asleep and unconcerned. But then Jesus arose, rebuked the storm, told peace to be still, and by that settled all their doubts... *that no problem is too big for God.*

So, it all comes down to faith, and what we choose to believe in this hour of American history. Do we believe God has abandoned us or that he is unconcerned? Or maybe we believe we have finally come up against a *cultural storm* that is too big for God to handle? Or maybe we think this whole plan to pray for the nation *and people who don't believe like us,* maybe we think that in this hour of American history we need a little something more *...like a good political strategy.*

Or just maybe some of us are finally getting the revelation, that we have not been praying for our nation, our fellow Americans, and our government leaders the way the Lord really intends for us to do. If churches in America routinely prayed like Timothy urged the early church to do ...*if we were regularly extending our faith for God's hand to be on our government,* I wonder if there would be so many in our midst who are fearful about the direction of our country.

Scripture is clear, the peace and prosperity of God's people are connected to the Lord's directive to pray for their government and its leaders ...*even if they don't think or worship like us.*

Look, his ego is inflated; he is without integrity. But the righteous one will live by his faith.
(Habakkuk 2:4)

A few months before the election, I watched a *YouTube* video posted by a noted pastor. The next day I got a notification that a comment I had posted, received some *likes* and a *reply*. The reply was engaging so I replied back, and then over the next several hours others chimed in and posted related comments. Well, someone shared a political opinion that didn't go over well with someone else on the thread, and before I knew it *the most hateful accusation* had been posted. Understand, this was a Christian video and for a while, we all sounded like Christians, but it was amazing how quickly everything changed and turned our digital fellowship into a *hate cave.*

Anyway, I turned off notification alerts and removed the video from my history, but the way a political opinion quickly changed the tenor of the conversation is something that has stuck with me until this day.

That experience was just a small taste of what I knew was going on all over the country on digital platforms like *Facebook* and *Twitter*. Leading up to the election, I had *unfollowed* a lot of people and deleted posts that offended me, but in all honesty, I am sure I *liked* and *shared* some posts that probably offended others. I never cursed anyone or made any nasty accusations, but it was hard not to get caught up in the political momentum of the last presidential election. Nevertheless, it was even harder for me to ignore the conviction of the Holy Spirit and *his call for me to turn it all off... everything. Delete the apps, fast the news... the Lord was telling me to turn it all off.* So, I did!

...note those who cause divisions and offenses, contrary to the doctrine which you learned, and avoid them.

(Romans 16:17)

Unleashing our anger on others, shaming our brothers and sisters in Christ, we can say we trust God and believe His Word, but in practice our actions are dividing His house. A house divided cannot stand. Not even Satan's kingdom can stand if it is divided against itself.[3] So we should understand that division in this country and the church is not a sustainable pursuit.

Look how good and how pleasant it is
when brothers live together in unity!
For there, the LORD commanded his blessing—
life everlasting.
(Psalm 133: 1 & 3)

The United States is by no means a pagan nation. In fact, we are probably known around the world as a Christian nation. It is probably

---

[3] Matthew 12:25-26

also true that the majority of politicians in this country identify as Christians, as do the majority of American voters. So, you would think it would be easy for Americans to agree in prayer to bless each other and the nation, but instead, we have been witnessing a hostile power struggle along political party lines. A power struggle that is seriously wounding the country and waxing boldly in the church. And for those who do not prioritize their walk with Christ over their politics, it also seems like we are witnessing an abandonment of *The Way* and *The Truth*.

> ***I urge you to*** *walk in a manner worthy of the calling you have received: with all humility and gentleness, with patience, bearing with one another in love, and with diligence to* ***preserve the unity of the Spirit through the bond of peace.***
> *(Ephesians 4:1-3)*

Preserving the unity of the Spirit through the bond of peace. It is an *about-face* for many of us, but it is the course correction and new end game that we all need right now. Unity is not an option for our nation or the church, it is our strength and salvation. Seeking peace and working to preserve unity is the condition connected to God's collective promise of a future and a hope for ourselves and America. It is *the only plan for people of faith* who know that God is the source of their security and hope *...and not the government.*

** ** ** ** **

So, what about you? Did you get caught up in the nasty momentum leading up to and following the last presidential election? Did you encounter any Christians dividing the Lord's house to win the vote? Do you think prayer and faith are the answer to the problems in our country or do you think we have finally come up against a cultural storm too big for God to handle? Honestly, what do you trust more... **your politics or Jesus**... *the One promising us a future and hope if we seek the peace of our nation?*

Chapter Two

Repent and Believe!

After John was put in prison Jesus came to Galilee, preaching the gospel of the kingdom of God, and saying, "The time is fulfilled, and the kingdom of God is at hand. Repent and believe in the gospel."
                                        (Mark 1:14-15)

CHRISTIANITY 101... the first things first... *the beginning of the Lord's ministry...* what we need to know, to consider, before we consider anything else. When I think about this verse from the gospel of Mark, I think about how very essential it is for all of us to do more than just believe the Gospel. Indeed, the Lord is telling all who will hear Him, to "*Repent ...and believe the Gospel!*

The Amplified Bible provides clarification about what the Lord is calling each of us to do by explaining that *repent* means to *have a **change of mind, regret for past sins,** and a **change of conduct for the better***. In other words, repent means more than just *I am sorry for what I did*, it really means that *I want to change what I am doing... I want to stop acting like this.*

...there will be more rejoicing in heaven over one sinner who repents than over ninety-nine righteous persons who do not need to repent.

(Luke 15:7)

When it comes to the way we have been doing politics in America we have to do more than just agree that it is tearing at the fabric of our nation and the church. *We need to stop acting like this*. More than acknowledging the big problem, as individuals we need to own the small part we play and the idea that *as Christians we have the power and obligation to mend the tear.*

The political relationship failure we see on a national scale has micro components being experienced as hostilities in the home, on social media, and in the way believers relate to one another in their communities. *Those quick to curse the darkness have become dark themselves*, but those willing to repent will find an opportunity to shine like brilliant lights at one of the darkest times in American history.

Owning relationship failure on an individual basis is no small thing. When I think about why human relationships fail, even why marriages fail, very often it is not a lack of love, loyalty, or willingness to forgive. No, more than anything else relationships fail because of a *lack of repentance*. The realization that a friend or a family member has no intention of changing the dysfunction that is damaging a relationship. The realization that *this is just how it is, this is all we can expect*. That realization is very often in the heart of the person who is walking away. And listen, the Lord tells us when it is wise to walk away.[4] After striving and *confrontations*, the Lord tells us, *"if he refuses to listen... let him be to you as an ...unbeliever."* (Matthew 18:17 AMP)

My Spirit shall not strive with man forever, for he is indeed flesh...
(Genesis 6:3)

Years ago, I had a friend who worked for a brash young professional who asked her to do a number of unscrupulous things *...including lying to his wife when she called the office.* One day my friend got up the courage to ask her boss if he was afraid he might go to Hell for the way he was living. *'No!'* he said, *'Right before I die... I plan to repent.'*

---

[4] Matthew 18: 15-17 AMP

*So what makes us think we can escape if we ignore this great salvation that was first **announced by the Lord Jesus himself**...*

(Hebrews 2:3)

As Christians, we would all like to believe our relationship with the Lord is secure... *not by our faithfulness to Him, but by His faithfulness to us.* When we consider the Gospel message of *abundant mercy* and *all-sufficient grace*, it's easy to convince ourselves that at the end of our lives all we will need to do is apologize and have faith in Jesus to save us. Most believers aren't as brash as my friend's former boss, but in practice... *in the way they do politics*, they seem to be living rebellious lives with faith in the same *scaled-down* version of Christianity. That in the end... sin, and the way they treated others won't really matter because all will be forgiven and obscured by their faith in Christ Jesus.

It sounds right ...but the big problem with *cheap grace is the idea that at the end of our lives, faith in Christ Jesus will be something that we can easily grasp.* Mental assent, or thinking you understand how salvation works, is different than *faith* that can appropriate that salvation to your own life of sin. In Matthew 18:17[5], Jesus compares the *hard-hearted unrepentant* man to an *unbeliever.* But more importantly, when Christ announced our great salvation, he said that he would suffer, die, and be resurrected in order to offer *"forgiveness of sins **for all who repent.**"*[6]

> *If we confess our sins, **he is faithful and just to forgive us our sins,** and cleanse us of our unrighteousness.*
>
> *(I John 1:9)*

---

[5] Matthew 18:17 AMP
[6] Luke 24:46-47 NLT

True grace is the knowledge that we don't deserve to be forgiven, but he is faithful to forgive us *anyway...because* he paid an **exorbitant price** for our sins when he died on the Cross. Our security in Christ is not that *our faith* obscures our sin. No, our security in Christ is that this *Great Merciful Lover who died for us*, is positioned to judge the world and forgive the sins of the world. *If* we confess our sins, *he is faithful and just to forgive us.* That forgiveness, that peace of mind, that security is available *now ...today when we repent and believe the good news of the gospel that we are forgiven.* Repentance is honest humility, the posture that moves the Lord to give us what we don't deserve. It is the way we come to the Lord and acknowledge that we need **the extravagant gift of salvation** that he is offering us today.

Jesus preached repentance, so who are we to cheapen his grace by taking it out of the equation? At a tremendous cost to himself, our Savior dealt with our sin, so it is not too much for him to ask us to deal with it as well. To *change our mind about it, to regret it,* and *change our conduct for the better.* Repentance *and faith that we are fully forgiven* is the way we appropriate salvation to our own life of sin. So, what makes *anyone believe* they can live any way they want and still escape by neglecting salvation ...*until they need it.*

*"Not everyone who says to Me, 'Lord, Lord,' shall enter the kingdom of heaven, but he who does the will of My Father in heaven. Many will say to Me **in that day**, 'Lord, Lord, have we not prophesied **in Your name**, cast out demons **in Your name**, and done **many wonders in Your name**?' And then I will declare to them, **'I never knew you;** depart from Me, **you who practice lawlessness**!'*

(Matthew 7:21-23)

Politics in America has evolved into an ugly dysfunctional affair...*a war to save the nation we love*, a failure of human relationships on a national scale. And yet somehow, we all know that the divisive way we do politics in the United States needs to change ...but it won't change unless we change. *Even so, many are asking, 'how can we disengage from this raging political battle when for so many of us, walking away feels like surrendering to evil?'*

*If my people who are **called by my name** will humble themselves and pray and seek my face and turn from their wicked ways, then I will hear from heaven and will **forgive their sin** and heal their land.*

(2 Chronicles 7:14).

Christians who genuinely know the Lord, know that *the way we feel is not His Gospel.* We also know that the Lord is not calling us to surrender to evil, he is calling us to surrender to *Him.* Those who know the Lord should be first to repent and believe the promise of *2 Chronicles 7:14*. We should be the first to understand that *God has not called anyone in the United States to engage in a bitter fight to save this nation*. On the contrary, God is asking his people to turn away from bitterness and seek Him *...so **He** can save our nation*[7].

Repent and believe the Gospel! The Lord is calling people who identify themselves as Christians *to stop trashing His grace, by acting as though the hateful way they talk about their fellow Americans is in line with His great commandment to love them.* Prayer is the small part we play in the fight to save our nation. And repentance is the way individual Christians can help mend what is tearing our nation apart. Those who are quick to curse the darkness will become even darker, but those willing to *repent* and *turn* from political hostility

---

[7] The battle is the Lord's ... (2 Chronicles 20:15)

will shine as brilliant lights at this dark hour in American history.

Let your light shine before others, that they may see your good works and give glory to your Father in Heaven,

(Matthew 5:16)

** ** ** ** **

So, what about you? Is it going to be business as usual... politics as usual? Or do you feel like the more you curse the darkness, the darker you get? Do you see yourself as a patriot in a war to save the nation you love? Or are you ready to surrender to faith? Who or what do you really believe can save our nation... **your politics or Jesus**, *the One who is calling everyone to surrender to him... so* **He** *can save our nation?*

Chapter Three

The Gatekeepers of Truth

Then the disciples came to Jesus and asked,
"Why do you speak to them in parables?"
(Matthew 13:10)

YOUR POLITICS OR JESUS, when I started thinking about this book, I began considering a number of scriptures I wanted to share. God and government can be found throughout the Bible and there are so many scriptures that can illuminate today's church. In any case, one day while I was reflecting on all this, I thought about the old Hans Christian Anderson folktale *The Emperor's New Clothes*. At first, I considered it to be just a random thought, but then I began to discern that there was something about that story that the Lord wanted me to see. So, I tried to recall all the details I could remember.

Two con men came to a town boasting they could weave a fabric so exquisite that only the worthy could see it. When the Emperor heard about this extraordinary fabric, he commissioned the two phony weavers to make him a royal garment. Not wanting to admit they were unworthy, the king and all his court pretended they saw the exquisite garment when in truth nothing was there. At one point the Emperor got so caught up in the delusion[8], that he dressed up in his new imaginary garments and paraded down the main street so everyone in town could see his new clothes. A child who wasn't concerned about impressing anyone, broke the spell when he said, 'The Emperor is naked!'

As I recalled the details of the story, I thought almost immediately that it was an old fable about a *cunning widespread deception*. I connected that idea to what some were reporting they

---

[8] Adherence to a peculiar belief that is contradicted by reality and rational thought.

experienced leading up to and following the 2020 presidential election. Many were talking about being led into *rabbit holes* of deception by groups peddling *online conspiracy theories*. Others were concerned that friends and beloved family members were caught up in the same kind of deception. One of the things I found particularly intriguing is that Christians seemed to be vulnerable and more notably involved than other groups.

Then there was the whole idea of election fraud. Many Americans believed it played a major role in the outcome of the presidential election, while many others characterized those claims as *The Big Lie*. To all that, add the fallout related to the numerous prophecies about the outcome of the election that did not pan out. One noted televangelist called the fallout *a big mess*. While several others were clearly preaching to a following that was disillusioned by what seemed like God's failure to show up.

For a while there was so much to ponder along these lines, so much to absorb, and yet I kept feeling like there was something in that classic old fable that would give me a revelation for this book. Finally, I pulled up a version of the original story on the internet.

A colorful old-world folktale, it was unfolding much as I had remembered. But then I read this passage, paraphrased below:

"I would really like to know how they are coming with the cloth!" thought the Emperor. But he was a bit uneasy when he recalled that anyone who was unfit for his position or stupid would not be able to see the material. Of course, he himself had nothing to fear, but still he decided to send someone else to see how the work was progressing.

*"I'll send my **honest old minister** to the weavers.... He is the best one to see how the material is coming. He is very sensible, and no one is more worthy of his position than he." So, the old minister went....*

"Goodness" thought the old minister, "I cannot see a thing. Gracious... Is it possible that I am stupid? Unfit for my office? No one must know this. It will never do for me to say I was unable to see the material." [9]

Almost as soon as I read it, I knew this passage was what the Lord wanted me to see. This story is not about a *cunning widespread deception*. This story is about the failure of the *gatekeepers of truth* to acknowledge a truth widely and clearly

---

[9] Hans Christian Andersen, Keisersens nye klaeder (1837). Translated by D.L. Ashliman)

perceived. There was nothing inherently trustworthy about the two con men who instigated the fraud. Andersen describes them simply as *scoundrels*. And that being the case, there was no plausible way that the deceivers would have been able to fool anyone, except for the fact that *the old minister affirmed the deception*.

After the minister lied and said he saw the garment, no one ...not even the King, had the confidence to trust their own eyes. The central antagonist in this story was not the two scoundrels, it was *the gatekeeper of truth* who failed to acknowledge the truth in his own eyes. The trusted man of God was more concerned with his royal appointment and reputation than he was about lying and the impact of his lie. The very thing he wanted to protect, *his reputation*, was the very thing that empowered the deception. The old minister didn't instigate the deception, but he empowered it when he affirmed it to the others.

"For judgment I have come into this world, so that the blind will see and those who see will become blind."

Some Pharisees who were with him heard him say this and asked, "What? Are we blind too?"

Jesus said, ***"If you were blind, you would not be guilty of sin; but now that you claim you can see, your guilt remains."***

(John 9:39-41)

"What? Are we blind too?" You can hear the Pharisees' contempt for what Jesus was saying here. And in the Lord's response to them, you can hear the seriousness with which he is warning them that they have a *really, big problem.* The Lord is saying, *your sin is not under my grace, because you claim you see the truth.*

The Pharisees were using their credentials as experts in the law and their reputation as gatekeepers of God's truth to influence the people to *reject the truth* and *their Savior*. It would have been one thing if they were wrestling with the scriptures and the testimony of the miracles, wrestling with honest doubts.[10] But the Lord knew that wasn't the case. The Lord knew that *if they had wanted to see the truth,* they could find it.[11]

But that's just it... the Pharisees *didn't want to see the truth.* They wanted to reject Jesus and they were *deceptively using their platform* as experts in the law to influence the people to have doubts about Jesus. So, *the One who sits in judgment of the world,* said to them, 'Because you *experts in the law* **claim to see...** I consider you to be **guilty**[12].'

---

[10] John 14:11

[11] *"Rabbi we know that you are a teacher sent by God, for no one can perform the signs you are doing unless God was with him."* John 3:2

[12] *". you have persuaded this nation to trust in lies."* Jeremiah 28:15-16

Now that is a problem. When the One you are trusting to forgive your sins by his grace... **when Jesus... considers you to be guilty**, *that is a really... big problem*.

> *Not many of you should become teachers, my brother, for you know that we who teach will be judged with greater strictness.*
>
> *(James 3:1)*

Like the old minister in the fable, the Pharisees *...the elite influencers of the Lord's people*, did not appear to have an in-depth understanding of the gravity of their sin. Pretending to see what was not there, denying what was there, and influencing people to *accept deception and reject the truth*. Apparently, they didn't understand the *enhanced consequences* of influencing others to believe deception... *but they should have*.

Mishandling *the truth*... the ministry of the Holy Spirit and influencing people to do the same thing, it is no small sin. *It is not under grace*, but it is an act inspired by Satan that makes the Lord angry.

From Heaven God shows how angry he is with all the wicked and evil things that sinful people do **to crush the truth.** *They know everything that can be known about God because* **God has shown it to them.** *...That's why those people don't have any excuse.*
(Romans 1:18-20 CEV)

The truth unacknowledged but widely and clearly perceived. The truth in your own eyes, the light Jesus gave you, the truth this verse in Romans says that God showed you himself which eliminates all your excuses. How did you handle *that truth* leading up to and following the last presidential election? How are you handling it now? Some elite influencers with significant platforms didn't handle the truth well. Some don't appear to be handling it well now. But those elite influencers *who for their audience* identify as Christians, have a really big problem and a guilty conscience that not even their *cheap grace* can fix.

Indeed, if they don't *repent now* ...and believe the gospel, if they don't try to locate themselves in John 9:39-41, what will they say on that day went they are *grasping for faith* in the One who identifies himself as *The Truth?*

'Lord, we prophesied **in your name** *and cast out demons* **in your name***. And oh, it got a little ugly, but we led the charge to save the nation from that other political party that was trying to run it into the ground. We did all that for you, Jesus. '*

Jesus answered, "Be careful that no one mislead you [deceiving you and leading you into error]."

(Matthew 24:4 AMP)

I love the fact that in Matthew 24:4 the Lord is exhorting **us** to take responsibility for what we choose to believe. Don't let anyone mislead you. Don't believe everything people tell you. Don't follow everyone who claims they are speaking for God. The Bible tells us clearly that we need to test the spirits ... and test the prophets. It warns us that many false prophets have gone out into the world. And it further tells us that when a prophet *"speaks in the name of the Lord, if the thing does not follow or come to pass,* **it is a word which the Lord has not spoken***, but the prophet has spoken it presumptuously.*[13]*"*

Follow me, as I follow Christ.

(I Corinthians 11:1)

---

[13] Deuteronomy 18:22

If you honestly have doubts and you want to know the truth, *check the inner witness of the Holy Spirit.* Because like *all* the characters in that old fable, *the truth might already be in your eyes.*

** ** ** ** **

So, what about you? Are you being careful to guard against deception? Do you want to know the truth? Do you trust the prophets even when they clearly get it wrong? Do you trust the gatekeepers of truth, more than you trust the light in your own eyes? And **what do you think the passion for politics in this nation is more about ...serving the souls of men or serving Jesus?** *But in any case, what are you serving...* **your politics or Jesus**, *the One who gave his life in service to all mankind?*

Chapter Four
Strong Delusion

Truly I tell you, anyone who will not receive the Kingdom of God like a little child, will never enter it.

(Luke 18:17)

IT IS INTERESTING that the hero of *The Emperor's New Clothes* is a little boy with no skin in the game. A child with no reputation to protect, and no clue why the adults were pretending. The child saw the truth and spoke the truth he saw, and with that *...the power of the delusion was broken.* The story ends by telling us that when the King heard the truth, he believed it and shuddered.

...they love the place of honor at banquets and the most important seats in the synagogues; they love

to be greeted with respect in the marketplaces and to be called 'Rabbi' by others.

(Matthew 23:6-7)

Jesus took his ministry directly to the people because the religious leaders of his day had too much drama going on. They were caught up in belonging to elite syndicates like the Pharisees and the Sadducees. They didn't want to offend the high priests or lose their prominent seats in the synagogues. They promoted themselves as being experts in the scriptures, but they didn't always obey the scriptures. For instance, Psalm 122 exhorts us all to *pray* for the peace of Jerusalem, but the religious leaders took it upon themselves to *orchestrate* the peace of Jerusalem with political strategies like killing Jesus and snuffing out his ministry. The religious leaders had too much skin in the game to acknowledge the truth about Jesus. Like the old minister in the fable, they had reputations to consider, and besides that, they feared what the Romans might do.

*If [only] you had known on this day [of salvation] ... the things which make for your peace [and on which peace depends]! For the time is coming when your enemies... will level you to the ground, you Jerusalem and your children within you..., all **because you did not recognize** the time of your visitation [when God was gracious toward you and offered you salvation]."*

(Luke 19:42-44 AMP)

They thought they were leading the charge to save the nation. They thought they were doing God a favor by opposing Jesus and his disciples. But the One who *accurately prophesied the destruction of Jerusalem*, said they had *no clue* about the things which made for their peace. Nor did they recognize the time of their visitation and God's gracious offer of salvation.

The coming of the lawless one will be accompanied by the working of Satan, with every kind of power, sign, and false wonder, and with every wicked deception directed against those who are perishing, **because they refused the love of the truth that would have saved them.** *For this reason, God will send them* ***a powerful delusion*** *so that they believe the lie, in order that* ***judgment may come upon all who have disbelieved the truth and delighted in wickedness.***
(2 Thessalonians 2:9-12)

These days politics can get us into so much trouble. It can inspire us to promote political strategies that divide the nation we claim to love and the church we claim to be building up. Our politics are inspiring us to express hatred toward those we should be loving, but more dangerously our politics are inspiring us to *delude ourselves into believing we have the flexibility to decide whose report we are going to believe.*

Deception is all about someone *tricking us* into believing something that is not true. *Delusion*, on the other hand, is about *our choice to believe* something that **contradicts reality** and *rational thought.* Delusion involves *our choice* to believe something that is not true, that doesn't line up with the facts. Moreover, delusion is adherence to a *peculiar or strange belief* that we or someone else made up, like *a garment so exquisite only the worthy can see it* or that *a golden calf represents the image of the Almighty God.*

A delusion is an argument or reasoning that exalts itself against the knowledge of God, the knowledge of the scripture. The higher reality of scripture tells us that ***we*** *are made in the image of God* and that we are not to make an idol in the form of anything on the earth to represent God. So, for those who are walking in the truth of scripture, it would not be *rational* to believe that a golden calf represents an image of the Almighty God.

*For we did not follow **cunningly devised fables** when we made known to you the power and coming of our Lord Jesus Christ, but we were **eyewitnesses** of His majesty.*
(2 Peter 1:16)

Faith in God is not a delusion. It is not a cunningly devised widespread deception. Unlike an *online conspiracy theory*, we are not making it up as we go. But our faith in God is founded on the proven reliability of scriptures that are thousands of years old. Our faith in God is founded on the testimony of saints that witnessed miracles and encountered God *in* reality.

Nevertheless, Christians are particularly vulnerable to delusion because our faith teaches us that we can *choose to believe* in a higher reality than what many people in the world can discern. Jesus, who we believe is the express image of God, on numerous occasions challenged the limits of reality and what most people could ever believe was possible. On one occasion a group of mourners told a man that his daughter was dead. Before he saw the girl or the man could say anything, Jesus said, *'That's not true, the girl is just sleeping.'* In response to what the Lord said, the mourners *laughed him to scorn.*

Now understand the mourners were simply trusting in *reality* as they believed it to be. The Lord, on the other hand, was creating a new reality with the words that he spoke. A new reality that everyone including the mourners would soon be able to discern and only explain as *a miracle.*

Miracles and delusions have this in common, *on the surface* it is not *rational* to believe either. However, in the case of *miracles only... if you know* the **Miracle Worker** ...and you know what *he wants* to do... and what *he is going to do*, then not only is it rational to believe in miracles, but it is also *our joyful hope.* But understand, you must both know *the Miracle Worker* ...and *his will.*

I tell you the truth, anyone who believes in me will do the same works I have done, and even greater works, because I am going to be with the Father.
(John 14:12)

The church has seen and will continue to see countless miracles because of the authority Jesus delegated to believers and because *he revealed the Father's will* on matters like salvation, healing, and deliverance. However, as the Lord was delegating authority to his disciples, they asked him when **he** would restore **the government** they were waiting for. In response, the Lord told them ...*it was not for them to know.* [14]

God had shown his *faithful prophet* Daniel his *times* and plans to reorder the world's governments and to bring forth his Messiah. Consistent with Daniel's prophecy, Jesus told his disciples, *"The Father alone has the authority to set those dates and times, and they are not for you to know".*[15]

> *"Blessed be the name of God forever and ever, for* **wisdom and power belong to Him,** *He changes the times and seasons;* **He removes kings and establishes them.**
>
> *(Daniel 2:20-21)*

When it comes to who will win a specific election in any given year, these are matters *under the*

---

[14] Acts 1:1-7
[15] Acts 1:7 NLT

Father's sole authority. God alone has the wisdom and power to remove and establish world leaders.[16] It is the Father's call *entirely*. Anyone walking in the light of the scriptures should know that even believers operating in *delegated authority*, do not have the **insight**[17] or the power to *agree, decree,* and *establish* a world leader. Jesus credited *his works ... his miracles* to the Father, so it is never *rational* to believe that apart from the Father's will, our faith can accomplish anything... *especially something Jesus told us was under the Father's sole authority.*

> *Behold,* ***they shall surely gather, but not by me....***
>
> *(Isaiah 54:14 KJV)*

---

[16] I Samuel 16:6-12
[17] ...the Lord does not see as man sees... the Lord sees the heart. (I Samuel 16:7)

Christ did not mislead his disciples when it came to the coming of the government they wanted to see. But he told them, *it was up to the Father.* So how is it that so many in today's church have developed an expectation that God should establish the government they want to see? And given that Christ told his disciples that such matters *weren't even for us to know*, don't you find it *peculiar* that an abundance of *prophecies claiming to know* God's will is a big reason people have developed so much fear and false hope around elections?

Beware of false prophets who come to you in sheep's clothing... You will know them by their fruit.
(Matthew 7: 15 and 20 NKJV)

Jesus always takes his ministry directly to the people because there is too much drama going on in high places. There are elite influencers all around us, online and in the church that have *no clue* what makes for our salvation or the peace of this nation. It is dangerous to believe these characters have *continuous access* to the Father's most confidential matters. *Matters that not even Jesus felt he should discuss.* It is dangerous to believe prophets have greater access to truth than the light in your own eyes *...especially when they keep getting it wrong.* Jesus said you will know a false prophet by *his fruit... by the inaccuracy of his prophecies.*

The choice to believe deception is delusion. As Christians, we choose to believe the Gospel. The two do not overlap, there is no gray area between the gospel and deception. *If we believe the gospel then we should be careful that no one deceives us.* We should want to know the truth and we should understand that there is no flexibility to believe anything else. When we take pleasure in the deception that's going around, when we repeat it and decide that is what we *prefer* to believe... and prefer that others believe, we are participating in and spreading strong delusion. That activity is not under the Lord's grace, but it is a practice inspired by Satan.

That little boy who is the hero of *The Emperor's New Clothes*, was not the hero because he was the only one who saw the truth. No every character in that old fable could see the truth, the little boy was the hero because he was the first who *acknowledged* the truth.

The truth unacknowledged but widely and clearly perceived. The truth in your own eyes, the light Jesus gave *you*, the truth Romans 1:18-20 says that God showed you himself which eliminates all your excuses. The truth that makes sense, that doesn't contradict the scriptures or the facts. How have you handled *that truth*? You may not be an elite influencer ...a politician, a prophet, someone with a large media platform; but somebody is watching you. And you need to understand that *you are a gatekeeper of the truth and the light that God has given you.*

Repent and believe the gospel! Because at this very hour the Lord is looking for heroes with no skin in the political games that are being played around them. Indeed, the Lord is looking for faithful gatekeepers, willing to speak the truth that others see but are unwilling to acknowledge because it conflicts with their agendas. Speaking the truth might not be a popular thing to do, but it will break the power of delusion in your circle and in the country. And when people hear the truth, *they will know it ...and may even shudder.*

** ** ** ** **

*So, what about you? Do you think the church has the wisdom to establish world leaders or do you think we should trust God to do that? And maybe you haven't instigated a deception, but you are wondering if on some level you affirmed it and participated in the delusion? And have you taken responsibility for what you choose to believe? If so, whose report will you believe, the one that facilitates **your politics or Jesus**... the One who came into the world to give us light?*

Chapter Five
A City or A Nation

Come, let us build ourselves a city, with a tower that reaches to the heavens, so that we may make a name for ourselves...." But the Lord came down to see the city and the tower the people were building."

(Genesis 11:4-5)

GOD AND GOVERNMENT, in the eleventh and twelfth chapters of Genesis we see God moving in two distinctly different ways. In the eleventh chapter, we see *men coming up with a plan and strategy* to build a tower, a city, and a name for themselves. A tower tall enough to reach the heavens was the strategy. People would come from far and wide to see it and in all that coming and going a city would be built and they would become famous. *It was a great plan, what could go wrong?*

Well, clearly God was not in the plan. There was nothing about it that honored Him or furthered His kingdom on earth. We know this because God had to come down to see what the men were doing. But instead of blessing their effort, *God frustrates it.*

The plans and strategies of men, when God is not a part of it, we can find ourselves frustrated and unfruitful. Even something as simple as an idea for a chapter in a book, if God is not in it, it's easier to push the delete button than to try and make it work. But if the Holy Spirit is moving, a little nudge to read an old folktale can turn into a revelation that can help us process what is going on around us.

I will make of you a great nation, and I will bless you and make your name great so that you will be a blessing. I will bless those who bless you, and him who dishonors you I will curse, and in you all the families of the earth shall be blessed."

(Genesis 12:2-3)

In the twelfth chapter of Genesis, we see God's plan to further His Kingdom on the earth when he calls Abraham, the Father of our Faith. This encounter with Abraham is the seed of *Judeo-Christianity*, a faith or *religion* that today has a major presence on every continent on earth. In the verse of scripture quoted above, God is sharing his plans for Abraham and the nations. God tells Abraham He is going to make him into a great nation, make his name great *so that* all the families of the earth would be blessed through him. And notice, *this is not Abraham's idea or strategy. This is God's plan*, a plan God himself will, and has brought to pass. All he needs from Abraham is *faith*.

> "**Cursed** is the man who trusts in man
> And makes flesh his strength,
> Whose heart departs from the Lord."
> "**Blessed** is the man who trusts in the Lord,
> And whose hope is the Lord."
>
> (Jeremiah 17: 5 and 7)

I love the contrast between the building of the *Tower of Babel* and *the call of Abraham*. The bigness of God's plans compared to the small-mindedness of men ...*it's amazing.* Both scenarios are about establishing a government in the earth, both plans speak of fame. However, the men building the Tower of Babel can only envision a tower and a city that would benefit themselves, whereas God spoke of a new nation that would bless the world. The men building Babel didn't have the power to make anything happen, and to this day there is no evidence that anything happened. Some historians consider this story to be a myth. Nevertheless, at the dawning of the twenty-first century, we can see the manifestation of what God promised to do. The faith of Abraham has spread to the four corners of the earth and three major religions claim him as the Father of their Faith.

> *"Our Father in heaven,*
> *hallowed be your name,*
> *your kingdom come,*
> *your will be done,*
> *on earth as it is in heaven.*
> *(Matthew 6:9-10)*

When Jesus taught His disciples to pray for God's Kingdom to come and His will to be done, he was telling them to buy into the big *and certain* plans that God has for this world. When we pray for God's kingdom to come and his will to be done, it is the most powerful prayer we can pray for ourselves and our nation. It is a prayer that brings us into partnership with God and His blessings.

Sure, it involves trusting God and walking by faith, but *isn't that how believers are expected to live? Isn't that the blessed life Jeremiah 17:7 speaks of? Still, walking by faith when you are not sure what God's will is... well, it isn't easy for any of us. It wasn't easy for Abraham, the Father of our Faith.*

When Abraham instinctively did God's will, when he made peace with his brethren, demonstrated bravery, showed hospitality to strangers, interceded for his neighbors, put his love and faith in God above his love for his son... those are the times when God showed up in a big way and blessed Abraham. By contrast, when Abraham was strategizing apart from God, when he walked in fear, lied about who his wife was, and abused his relationship with his maidservant, God wasn't a part of Abraham's *carnal strategies*. And as a result, a trail of sorrow and resentment followed the prophet and his family, a trail that some believe lingers in Middle East tensions today.

And Jesus replied to him, "'You shall love the Lord your God with all your heart, and with all your soul, and with all your mind.' This is the first and greatest commandment. The second is like it, 'You shall love your neighbor as yourself [that is, unselfishly seek the best or higher good for others].' **The whole Law and the [writings of the] Prophets depend on these two commandments."**
(Matthew 22:37-40 AMP)

I love the scripture quoted here because it says essentially if you don't know the *Ten Commandments* by heart or all the do's and don'ts in your Bible, choosing to love God with all your heart, mind, and soul and choosing to love your neighbor as yourself is *the best strategy to follow.*

Jesus said all the laws and the prophets depend on those two commandments, so *how can you miss the will of God if you aim to love God and your neighbors.* And when it comes to an election, doing God's will shouldn't be about some spooky ethereal, *thus sayeth the Lord revelation* of God's chosen one, as much as it should be about the way we choose to behave toward our fellow Americans.

> *For where there are envy, strife, and division among you, are you not carnal and behaving like mere men? For when one says,* ***I am of Paul****, and another,* ***I am of Apollos****, are you not carnal and acting like mere men?*
>
> *(I Corinthians 3:3-4)*

She is a Republican. He is a Democrat. Which one is good? Which one is evil? Unfortunately, these days there are too many among us who believe they can answer those questions? Even though,

Jesus said things like, *'Who made me a judge over you? And why do you call me good? Only God is good.'* Even though the Bible teaches us that *The Almighty despises no one*[18], it is amazing how many Christians are quick to judge, quick to get angry, and closed to political views that challenge their own.[19]

It is obvious that God is not in that type of behavior, but what is not so obvious is that those dark offensive people are precisely who we should be praying for. When we humble ourselves and pray for the healing of our nation, the people who offend us the most are the faces we should see. Praying for those who have been wounded by politics is the small part we play as change agents for peace.

---

[18] Job 36:5
[19] *...be quick to hear, slow to speak, slow to get angry -.* James 1:19

*You have heard that it was said, love your neighbor and hate your enemy. But I tell you to **love your enemies and pray for those who persecute you...***

. *(Matthew 5:43-44)*

It is not instinctive to do God's will and to bless people who have grown dark. But if we respond by cursing them, their trail of sorrow will begin to follow us. However, when we forgive and pray for their healing, God will show up for us in a big way.

*But the fruit of the Spirit is love, joy, **peace**, longsuffering, gentleness, goodness, faith...*

(Galatians 5:22-23)

Over the years, elections and the state of the nation have been substantial concerns of my prayer life. In my talks with Jesus, I have revealed my heart and thoughts about how I planned to vote. I have offered the Lord my vote. I have asked him not to ask me to vote for certain candidates that I didn't believe in. I have asked him to favor candidates I did believe in. And *with the full knowledge that what I wanted, might not be what God wanted,* I still prayed for *His will* to be done in the outcome of elections. As such, I have been disappointed by election results, but on other occasions, I have celebrated election results. However, since I believe *no man can receive anything unless it has been given to him by God the Father*[20], I believe that whether I understand it or not, the person that God wants to occupy an office for any given term is the person who won the election. I may be

---

[20] John 3:27

disappointed with election results, but I am never disappointed in God *because it is **His call entirely.***

> *Let every soul be subject to the governing authorities.* ***For there is no authority except from God****, and the authorities that exist are **appointed** by God.*
>
> *(Romans 13:1)*

Second Chronicles 7:14 is a call for the people of God to humble themselves, repent and pray for the nation. For me, that is not a call for a single prayer or several prayers right before an election. For me, that refers to the *ongoing peaceful conversations* that I have had with Jesus over the years about our country and the world. In that prayer relationship, I have developed faith in God's love for me and all people. And I have also experienced the conviction of the Holy Spirit *to repent* about the wrong way I sometimes do politics, times when I criticized leaders that I should have prayed for.

Interesting though, *I have been a spirit-filled Christian for more than 20 years, and never once has the Holy Spirit tried to influence my vote. Nevertheless, there seems to be no shortage of political influencers in the Church. Some of whom, have been agreeing and decreeing in faith to see their will done in elections.*

*This is the confidence we have in approaching God, that if we ask anything **according to his will**, he hears us...*

(I John 5:14)

** ** ** ** **

So, what about you? What do you think reflects God's sovereign will in an election year, those special prophetic words telling you how to vote or his great commandment to love our fellow Americans? And do you think you can tell who is good and who is evil based on their political party affiliation? Or do you think people who judge other people like that are the ones with the real problem? And who or what do you think can influence the vote more... **your politics or Jesus**, *the One who is able to make all grace abound toward every good work?*

A Prayer for Godly Government Servants

Lord raise up godly leaders in pursuit of Your Righteousness who will glorify You in their victories and their service to the nation and the world.

In Jesus Name,

Amen!

L. C. Brown Bush

Chapter Six

The Religious Political Strategy

*Then I hated all my labor in which I had toiled under the sun, because I must leave it to the man who will come after me. And **who knows whether he will be wise or a fool**? Yet he will rule over all **my labor** in which I toiled and in which I have shown myself wise under the sun.*
(Ecclesiastes 2:18-19)

I THINK IT IS INTERESTING that in this passage of scripture Solomon expressed anxiety over leaving his kingdom to his son Rehoboam. I think Solomon knew Rehoboam didn't have what it took to rule the kingdom he worked so hard to build. Years later, consistent with Solomon's fears, his son's leadership abilities were tested almost immediately after he ascended to his father's throne. In the first critical decision of his reign, Rehoboam had a choice between following the advice of the elders who had helped his father build the kingdom or following the advice of his young friends who had never built anything.

Rehoboam made the wrong decision and in one day, ten of the twelve tribes of Israel abandoned his kingdom and initiated the process of forming a new government under the rulership of *Jeroboam*, the first king of the Northern Kingdom, often referred to as **Samaria.**

Jeroboam said in his heart, "Now the kingdom might revert to the house of David. ***If these people go up to offer sacrifices in the house of the LORD at Jerusalem,*** *their hearts will return to their lord, Rehoboam king of Judah; then they will kill me and return to Rehoboam king of Judah. After seeking advice, the king made* **two golden**

> ***calves*** *and said to the people, "Going up to Jerusalem is too much for you.*
>
> *Here, O Israel, are your gods, who brought you up out of the land of Egypt."*
> (I Kings 12:26-28)

As they were forming their new government Jeroboam immediately saw a problem. *The Temple, ...the worship center of his people,* was in Jerusalem, which was still under the control of their former king, Rehoboam. If the people made regular pilgrimages to worship at the Temple in Jerusalem, *Jeroboam feared* they might soon reunite with their brethren in Judah and renew their allegiance to their former king. *For that reason*, Jeroboam came up with a **religious political strategy** designed to preserve his power and strengthen the Northern Kingdom. **It was in Jeroboam's political interest to keep the people**

divided, so he came up with a new religion, new worship centers, and *a new god... a golden calf.*

After reading the last chapter, I hope you know enough about the seed of Judeo-Christianity to see all the red flags associated with Jeroboam's *religious political strategy*. He doesn't even pray about it, but after consulting with *other men*, Jeroboam comes up with a plan ...*to start a new religion??? Really???*

Jeroboam started *a new religion* that benefited his little political group and their ambitions. *Do you think God was in that*[21]? And the saddest part about this *new hybrid religion* is how much it contradicted his people's longstanding faith in the God of Abraham, Isaac, and Jacob.

---

[21] I Kings 13:1-9

Jeroboam, and the Israelites who followed him down that *rabbit hole* of delusion, had apparently forgotten their history and scriptures. They had forgotten that when the Hebrews were delivered out of Egyptian bondage, and Moses was on Mount Sinai getting the *Ten Commandments*, the people fashioned *a golden calf* and said *that* was the god who had delivered them out of Egyptian bondage. Hundreds of years later, that is exactly what Jeroboam told the people in the newly formed kingdom of Samaria. But what he didn't tell the people, maybe because *he didn't know or care,* is that the worship of the golden calf greatly offended God and brought *a plague* and death into the Hebrew camp[22]. Indeed, when Moses heard the Israelites worshiping the golden calf, he called it the *sound of defeat.*

Go, tell Jeroboam that this is what the LORD, the God of Israel, says: 'I raised you up from among the

---

[22] Exodus 32:1-35

people and appointed you ruler over My people Israel. I tore the kingdom away from the house of David and gave it to you. But **you were not like My servant David**, *who kept My commandments and followed Me with all his heart, doing only what was right in My eyes.*

You have done more evil than all who came before you. **You have proceeded to make for yourself other gods and molten images to provoke Me, and you have flung Me behind your back.** *Because of all this, behold, I am bringing disaster on the house of Jeroboam.*

(I Kings 14:7-10)

Like King David, Jeroboam was a mighty man of valor who God chose to be the first king of the Northern Kingdom. Appointed, *but not anointed* to be king, the prophet Ahijah told him that *if* he served God with all his heart the way King David had, that God would give him an *enduring* kingdom. However, unlike King David, Jeroboam was not interested in pursuing God's heart or doing what was right in God's sight. Jeroboam was only interested in pursuing *raw political power* ...so much so that he invented a god and flung the True and Living God behind his back. **Jeroboam is an anti-Christ figure.** *The fool that failed the third temptation of Christ,* as one who sold his soul and the soul of God's people to the Devil in exchange for a *temporal earthly kingdom.*

Only the Almighty can offer an enduring kingdom and everlasting life. Satan has nothing more to offer man than *a time slot in his short reign on earth.*[23] So understand, Jeroboam chose *fleeting fame and political power* over the enduring kingdom that God was offering him. Later, the prophet Ahijah sent this message from the Lord to Jeroboam, *"You have done more evil than all who came before you."*

---

[23] Revelation 12:12

> ***Why do the nations rage,***
> *And the people plot a vain thing?*
> *The kings of the earth set themselves,*
> *And the rulers take counsel together,*
> *Against the* Lord *and against His Anointed...*
>
> *(Psalm 2:1-2)*

So how was he able to do it? How did Jeroboam lead the people of God into a *strong delusion* and away from the One True God? *Well ...they were angry! And they had been angry for a long while.*

The people were *blinded by their anger* over Solomon's taxes and his son's callous attitude toward their request to modify those taxes. The people had been seething over their taxes for years even when Solomon was still alive. **Jeroboam used the anger and indignation of the people to position himself** to rule the Northern Kingdom. However, hundreds of years after the demise of Jeroboam's kingdom and the kingdom of Judah, the hostility that divided the House of Israel was still burning hot and blinding the people of God.

> ***Jesus replied***, *"...a time is coming when you will worship the Father neither on this mountain nor in Jerusalem. You **Samaritans** worship what you do not know; we worship what we do know, for salvation is from the Jews. Yet a time is coming and has now come when the **true worshipers will worship** the Father **in the Spirit and in truth**, for they are the kind of worshipers the Father seeks.*
> *(John 4: 21-23)*

Fast forward almost a thousand years *after* Jeroboam instituted his *hybrid religion* in Samaria. Jesus is born at a time when the hostility between Jews and Samaritans is entrenched in the culture and both sides are comfortable with the division. Little Jewish children were raised with the understanding, *we hate Samaritans, and we don't speak to them.* Likewise, Samaritan children were raised with a similar disdain for Jews. When Jesus appears on the scene, the opposition is so sharp that he finds himself speaking to the divide on several occasions. In John 4:22, a Samaritan woman the Lord meets at a well, asks him to give his take on what was at the *root* of the longstanding divide between Samaritans and Jews. In a *bold and truthful* response Jesus tells the woman, *You Samaritans worship what you do not know. Salvation is from the Jews.*

Essentially, the Lord is telling her *the truth*, that her salvation is not found in *the religious political strategy* that her forefather *Jeroboam initiated.* Salvation is found in that faith relationship that *God initiated* with his people, that started when He called Abraham and that was perfected in the life, death, and resurrection of Jesus Christ. *The faith we find in scripture.*

Again, the historical and cultural disdain between Jews and Samaritans was so prevalent in the Lord's day, that it is often compared to *racial hatred* even though both groups traced their bloodline back to Abraham, Isaac, and Jacob. On one occasion, one of his disciples asked Jesus if he wanted them to call down fire on the Samaritans like Elijah had done when he confronted the prophets of Jezebel. In response, Jesus rebuked his disciple and said, *"You don't know what spirit you are of!"* [24]

On another occasion, Jesus makes a clear connection with the commandment to love your neighbor and the parable known as the *Good Samaritan*. That same connection is central to the saving grace the Lord has made available to America, to help heal the *current* cultural divide along political party lines.

---

[24] Luke 9:51-55

*One day an expert in the law stood up to test Him. "Teacher," he asked, "what must I do to **inherit eternal life**?" "What is written in the Law?" Jesus replied. "How do you read it?"*

*He answered, "'Love the Lord your God with all your heart and with all your soul and with all your strength and with all your mind and '**Love your neighbor as yourself**.' "*

You have answered correctly," Jesus said. *"Do this and you will live."*

*But **wanting to justify himself**, he asked Jesus, "And who is my neighbor?"*

(Luke 10:25-29)

They didn't know. Jesus said the Samaritans *didn't know* what they were worshiping. And even though many of the Jews thought their hatred for Samaritans was justified, the Lord rebuked his disciples because the Jews *didn't know* what spirit was driving them to hate Samaritans. If we think about it, we can see the same *blind dynamics* at work in the sharp divide between Democrats and Republicans in the United States? Many believe that the disdain they feel for people who identify with the political party they oppose is justified. Like the Lord's disciples who were offended by Samaritans, many Christians caught up in today's political hostilities think Jesus is just as offended as they are by some of the political ideologies that Americans adhere to.

Not long ago, I was watching a *YouTube* video in which a pastor said to his congregation, *Jesus is not a Republican. He is not a Democrat. He's not even an American.* When I heard that obvious true statement, I wondered why it has become necessary to say that to Christians in a *modern* American church. Are Christians *conveniently blind* about what is at the heart of the political hostilities in the United States? The truth widely perceived but unacknowledged by many in the church is that,

It is in the political interest of some pursuing power in our government to encourage hostility and division along political party lines. Because the majority rules, the quest for **political party domination** *is at the heart of the strategies that are dividing our country and fueling political hostilities. It is an ongoing struggle because it involves the pursuit of* **temporal earthly power**.

Many in the church have gotten so wrapped up in these political hostilities that they have become conveniently blind to the way the *Jeroboam spirit* contradicts the pillars of the Christian faith. They conveniently ignore the fact that the election outcomes they are *fighting* about, are not enduring nor are they worth compromising the pursuit of eternal life in Christ Jesus.

Can two walk together without agreeing where to go?

(Amos 3:3)

Have some Christians forgotten who Christ is? Are some of us out of step with His Word and how it prioritizes *love* and connects it to our eternal salvation? *What spirit is driving Americans to hate other Americans who don't vote like them?* Have we gotten so entrenched in the political loyalties we grew up with, that we can't follow Jesus... *even though we claim he is following us?*

** ** ** ** **

So, what about you? Does your anger and opposition to a political party take precedent over your love walk with Jesus? Do you think it is possible to be loyal to a political party and at the same time be loyal to Christ? Or is **priority** *a better word for the way you manage politics and your faith? And if* *so, have you ever had to decide which to follow...* **your politics or Jesus**, *the One helping us to hear the sound of defeat in our political camps?*

** ** ** ** **

The LORD hasn't lost his powerful strength.
He can still hear and answer prayers.
Your sins are the roadblock.
between you and your God.
That's why He doesn't answer your prayers or let you see His face.
(Isaiah 59:1-2 CEV)

Chapter Seven
The Seat of the Scornful

*Watching for their opportunity, the leaders sent spies **pretending to be honest men.** They tried to get Jesus to say something **that could be reported** to the Roman governor so he would arrest Jesus. "Teacher," they said, "we know that you speak and teach what is right and are not influenced by what others think. You teach the way of God truthfully. Now tell us—**is it right for us to pay taxes to Caesar or not**?"*

He saw through their trickery *and said, "Show me a Roman coin....*

(Luke 20:20-24)

TAXES... the people were *angry* about oppressive taxes. It was a hot political topic in Rehoboam's day and *hundreds of years later Jesus* would also face a critical test about *the same hot political topic*. When Rehoboam inherited the kingdom, he didn't know how it worked. He thought the kingdom his father Solomon built was held together by force, by his father's army. He had no idea how important the peoples' cooperation was to his success as king. Rehoboam and his friends were benefiting from the tax system that his father had imposed, so when his subjects asked him to modify it. Rehoboam, influenced by his friends, refused to listen to the people. In fact, trying to show how tough he was, Rehoboam threaten to raise taxes even more. That was the first and last decision he would make as ruler of his father's entire kingdom. Because *of that one callous decision*, ten of the twelve tribes of Israel deserted him and form their own nation under Jeroboam.

Jesus by contrast fully understood what his Father needed him to accomplish for the Kingdom of God. He also fully understood what the Pharisees were up to when they tried to trick him into publicly expressing his opinion about the oppressive tax system imposed by the Romans. *Jesus came to die... to give his life for the salvation of mankind.* And he was eventually killed at the hands of Roman executioners. Before it all happened, he told his disciples multiple times that he would be crucified at the hands of evil men... and he knew exactly who those evil men were. So, in this critical test the Lord was not concerned about his own life and safety... *he was concerned about accomplishing the Father's sovereign will.*

But so we don't cause offense...
(Matthew 17:27)

Jesus had an opinion... *an unfavorable opinion about the oppressive tax systems of his day...* but more importantly he had a mission to accomplish for his Father. The Lord did not come to die as a political martyr... he came to die as the *Lamb of God* for the sins of the world. So, he paid his taxes, kept his political opinions private[25], and with the wisdom of God outsmarted the lame attempts by his enemies to entrap himself *publicly* with his own words. But beyond just watching what he said in public, *Jesus appeared to have no interest in politics.* Genuinely and by design, Jesus showed no interest in addressing the *fleeting concerns of the government* empowered at the time, but his *total focus* was putting in place eternal salvation for all mankind.

> *Jesus... said to them, "All authority (all power of absolute rule) in heaven and on earth has been given to Me. Go therefore and* **make disciples of all the nations [help the people to learn of Me, believe in Me, and obey My words]**, *baptizing them in the name of the Father and of the Son and*

---

[25] Matthew 17:24-27

of the Holy Spirit, **teaching them to observe everything that I have commanded you;** *and lo, I am with you always ...even to the end of the age."*

(Matthew 28:18-20 AMP)

The Great Commission, if anything sums up the focus and mission of Christian believers and the church, the Lord's final words to his disciples before he ascended into Heaven lays it out clearly. Christians are supposed to disciple the nations, by teaching them to observe the commandments that the Lord has commanded us to observe. Our focus should be the salvation and discipleship of our family and communities not the manipulation of their vote. Furthermore, if keeping our opinions about *hot political topics* to ourselves advances the Kingdom of God, then like the Lord, we need to prioritize what is more *important ...influencing people around us to vote like us or influencing them to give their life to Christ to a greater degree.*

A faithful saying that most Christians have heard that should inspire all of us to live out our faith is, *'maybe the only Jesus some people will ever see, is the Jesus lived out in me.'* That faithful saying is consistent with what the Lord told his disciples in John 13:35, that essentially people will know that we are his disciples *by the love we have for one another.* On the other hand, I think it is also true, that people will know that *we have lost our way* when our testimony reveals that we have prioritized our personal interest and political agendas over our call to serve Christ.

> *"You are so proud of knowing the law, but you dishonor God by breaking it. No wonder the Scriptures say, "The Gentiles blaspheme the name of God because of you."*
> *(Romans 2: 23-24)*

Many *unbelievers* say that the reason they reject Christianity is because of the hypocrisy they see lived out in people who claim to be Christians.

Mahatma Gandhi, very famously said, *"I like your Christ, but not your Christianity."* Gandhi said he read his Bible *"faithfully"*, but he also said that he thought Christians were *"the most warlike people."*[26] When you think about the warlike way many Americans are doing politics these days, what do you think we are affirming to the unbelievers that are watching. Are we affirming Gandhi's observations to the nations Christ told us to disciple? If so, that is a huge dilemma for the modern church, because our political hostilities and hypocrisy get a lot more coverage than our efforts to love one another.

Do you not know that friendship with the world is hostility toward God? Therefore, whoever chooses

---

[26] *Mahatma Gandhi Says He Believes in Christ, But Not Christianity*, Anonymous, January 11, 1927; https://www.thecrimson.com/article/1927/1/11/mahatma-gandhi-says-he-believes-in/

to be a friend of the world renders himself an enemy of God.

(James 4:4)

Honestly, I don't know what is more sinister, our own hypocrisy or the hypocrisy we justify in the people we choose to follow. Maybe it is one and the same, as scripture admonishes us not to deceive ourselves, *"bad company corrupts good character.*[27]*"*

I shared earlier, that I haven't always done politics right. But since the central way I do politics is in the Lord's presence on my knees, the Holy Spirit has been able to convict me about the way that I have criticized leaders I should have been praying for. In the light of prayer, the Lord showed me that part of the reason I was so critical, is because *the news commentaries I was watching were similarly*

---

[27] I Corinthians 15:33

critical. For me to repent, I had to turn off and end my fellowship with *negative news commentary.*

We cannot have it both ways, James tells us whoever chooses friendship with the world chooses to be an enemy of God. Psalm 1:1 which has been key to bringing about my personal repentance, says that the blessed person *does not* walk in the counsel of the *ungodly.* **The blessed person does not sit in the seat of the scornful.** The blessed person *does not* stand in the path of sinners.

> *I urge you to walk in a manner worthy of the calling you have received: with all humility and gentleness, with patience, bearing with one another in love, and with diligence to* **preserve the unity of the Spirit through the bond of peace.**
>
> *(Ephesians 4:1-3)*

Don't get me wrong, the *free press* is essential to democracy. It is an important part of the checks and balances that keep us all honest and makes America one of the greatest countries in the world. When men and women *of integrity, with integrity,* keep us informed and share balanced commentaries about issues and events that impact the citizens of this country and the world, *we are all blessed and benefited by their service.* But when these elite influencers sit in the *seat of the scornful* and mishandle the truth, those of us who can discern *the spirit of Jeroboam* at work in their motives, need to turn them off and hold them accountable to the noble standards afforded to them by our Constitution.

But it's not just news commentaries, *the spirit of Jeroboam that is sowing division through hostility* on the national stage is showing up in hostilities in our homes, on social media, and in our communities. In some instances, we may be able to just turn off or avoid corrupting influences, but in other instances, we may need *divine intervention*.

> *If we confess our sins, he is faithful and just to forgive us our sins, and **cleanse us of our unrighteousness**.*
>
> *(I John 1:9)*

Years ago, I had a debilitating addiction to cigarettes. I tried everything to get free, quitting cold turkey, hypnosis, acupuncture, you name it, I tried it, but nothing stuck. Then one morning shortly after I had received *the baptism of the Holy Spirit*, I made a tearful apology to the Lord. I told him I was sorry that I had abused my body with cigarettes, and I told him I thought my life would probably be cut short because I was addicted to smoking and couldn't stop. Later that same day someone who had no idea that I had tearfully repented that morning, prayed for me to quit smoking. That was over twenty years ago, *and I haven't smoked a cigarette since that prayer.*

That experience taught me about the power of repentance and confessing my sin. First John 1:9 promises that if we confess our sin, God is faithful and just to forgive us... *but it promises something more.* It promises **divine intervention**... that **God will cleanse us** of *our unrighteousness.* After I sincerely repented, because *of that promise of divine intervention*, God delivered me from an addiction I couldn't overcome on my own.

Listen, *we don't always have the ability to change* ourselves or our circumstances *but that should not stop us from repenting and changing our mind about our sin.* When we sincerely confess our sin, we tap into the Lord's promise to cleanse us of our unrighteousness. That divine intervention might not manifest itself in a same day miracle like it did for me ...but over time if you want to be free of your unrighteousness, you will see the power of

God cleansing you and helping you get free. So, if you find yourself seated in the *seat of the scornful*, stop justifying that angry critical spirit, change your mind about it, confess it as sin, and then trust God to help you get free.

** ** ** ** **

So, what about you? Do you know what spirit you are of? Do you feel justified by your anger or do you feel like you need divine intervention to get free? Do you have any influences in your life that are corrupting your good conduct... your good communication? And when it comes to pursuing political party loyalty or the bond of unity through peace, what will you choose... **your politics or Jesus**... *the One known as the Prince of Peace?*

Chapter Eight

Don't Be Conformed

*And when they saw it, **they all grumbled**, "He has gone in to be the guest of a man who is a sinner."*

(Luke 19:7)

JESUS WAS NEVER *politically correct.* He was always making friends with the wrong people. Going to the wrong parties and saying nice things about people other people *hated.* He didn't care what the religious leaders thought… but then again, he didn't care about what the crowds thought either. It was bad enough that he used *a Samaritan* as a good example when he was teaching, but when he hung out with *tax collectors* …consistently! Ugh! Nobody was happy about that.

At this point many of his disciples turned away and deserted him."

(John 6:66)

Jesus, the *uncompromising nonconformist,* the radical *activist* from the kingdom of God... Jesus wasn't going to let anyone use him to get what they wanted. Nor was he about to say what the crowds wanted him to say so they would keep coming back. Jesus was not a people pleaser, a politician looking for votes, a news anchor looking for ratings, or a *TikToker* looking to go viral. He wasn't trying to get accepted by the cool kids that were haters. *Nor was he concerned about his own reputation.*

Jesus came to show us the way of eternal salvation. It wasn't always a popular message, but it is the truth, we all need to hear.

Everybody wants what Jesus has to offer... but not everyone is willing to walk with him to the end.

> *Are you also going to desert me?*
> *Simon Peter replied, Master to whom shall we go, for* ***you alone have the words of eternal life****. And we believe them and know you are the Holy Son of God. Then Jesus said, I chose the twelve of you, and one of you is **a devil**.*
> *(John 6:67-70)*

The *spirit of Jeroboam* has no interest in trying to figure out how to please God and pursue his political ambitions. That spirit will have you thinking that *'Politics is a dirty game, that's just how it is. That's just how we roll in the United States...* **divide** *and conquer. Worry about Jesus later when you need him but right now ...get real... pursue the vote!'* That foolish anti-Christ spirit will build a golden calf to make you think he's religious, but in truth he has no problem choosing this temporal life over eternal life and his politics over Jesus. *But what about you? Are you following Jeroboam's delusion?[28] Do you have Jesus on hold?*

> *And **do not be conformed to this world**, but be transformed by the renewing of your mind, that you may prove what is that good and acceptable and perfect will of God.*
>
> *(Romans 12:2)*

Jesus is Christianity. His life, his doctrine, his faith, his miracles, his choices, his resurrection, his purpose... all of that is the substance of the eternal life we need from him *right now*. All of that is what it means to be a Christian. Anyone can take on any title they want? Anyone can say they are a Christian or a Republican or a Democrat. And

---

[28] *Come eat with me and I will give you a gift.* - I Kings 13:1-7

many people take on these titles just so they can influence people or so they can belong.

But Jesus, the *uncompromising non-conformist* is asking those who belong to him to be zealous *first* for the Kingdom of God. The Lord is asking his followers *not to conform to this world* and the divisive hostility that has come to characterize American politics. Instead, the Lord is asking us to **work diligently to preserve unity**... the unity of his church and the unity of our nation *...through the bond of peace.*

> ***Seek ye first the kingdom of God*** *and his righteousness, and all these things will be added unto you.*
>
> *(Matthew 6:33)*

I reviewed several definitions of the word *politics* before I chose the one I used at the beginning of this book. That definition stood out to me because it describes politics in terms of *activity*. The activity of government. The activity concerned with government policy. The activity concerned with the control of government. Almost all of us are wrapped up with these concerns. To some extent maybe most Americans would describe themselves as *political activists* concerned with what they believe is best for our nation.

From peaceful protests to domestic terrorism, from winning just one other vote to starting a movement, most Americans consider *their brand of political activism* to be an honorable pursuit. But like any activity, those of us on the outside looking in aren't easily persuaded. From the outside looking in we can discern corruption and less than honorable motives. But also from that perspective, we can find ourselves buying into what we believe to be true and noble causes. Political activism in and of itself is not a bad thing. In fact, *the Holy Spirit calls some of us into that space.* However, like those attempting to build the Tower of Babel, selfish ambition and pride are what call others to action. From the outside looking in, we can discern *nobility* and from that same vantage point, we can also discern when the Holy Spirit is nowhere in political activities.

For those in the church who have gotten wrapped up in the most egregious practice of *false prophecy*, it seems like their political activism is what has led them astray. Then there are those *mining votes in the church* who love to talk about the nobility of their political views. They are in the fight to save the nation for Jesus. They vote their Christian conscience and can't understand how anyone who calls themselves a Christian can vote for *him... or her.*

> *...seek ye **first** the kingdom of God, and his righteousness...*
>
> (Matthew 6:33)

The extent to which our political activism comes first is the extent to which we can compromise the church and the priorities that Christ set for us. It is the extent to which we are pursuing our righteousness as opposed to His.

...Go ye into all the world and preach the gospel to every creature. He that believeth and is baptized shall be saved; but he that believeth not shall be damned.

(Mark 15:15-16)

The unchurched, those who have never heard the gospel, those we should be witnessing to, those most in need of Christ ...we shouldn't be surprised when politics is their priority and most honorable pursuit. However, when *political activism becomes the priority of Christians, we are setting conditions on our relationship with the lost and dying world.* There are those who need to hear our wisdom and testimony, who will never hear it because we are leading with political activity that turns them off. But even more awkwardly, how are we going to convince anyone to make Jesus their priority when they can clearly see he's not ours. And if they die in their sins because we failed to do our job, what are we going to say on that day when we are grasping for faith in the One who died for them. The One holding *us* accountable for their souls.[29]

Repent and believe the Gospel!

The vote is so uncertain. It promises us nothing... but the hope that our political aims might reign for *a season.* And yet in pursuit of it, some have lost their focus on the priorities Christ set for us. The priority to edify the saints around us and preach the Gospel to a lost and dying world.

---

[29] Ezekiel 33:8

The apostasy... *the great falling away of the church.*[30] Many believe it will be characterized by a lack of interest in *the Faith*, but maybe it is shaping up to look like *a more intense interest* in other things... *like politics.*

** ** ** ** ** **

So, what about you? Is your political activism your most honorable pursuit? **Do you have Jesus on hold?** *Have you invested too much hope in the uncertain promise of the vote? Do you think we will ever learn to bring our concerns about our government to God first ...to do our political activism on our knees?* **Your politics or Jesus?** *Don't you think that is a question we should all revisit regularly as we actively love America and work to preserve its unity through the bond of peace?*

---

[30] *...the one who now restrains it will continue until he is taken out of the way...* (2 Thessalonians 2:5-7)

L. C. Brown Bush

Conclusion

Call to Prayer

THIS CALL TO PRAYER that we have been neglecting. That we don't think is enough to effectively deal with our current cultural storms. This prayer that *we measure its effectiveness by* what we see or the outcome of elections. This prayer... this faith... this intimate relationship with *The Truth*, even the unity and agreement of believers... these are just a small part of the arsenals and defense weaponry of *that great army... the Church.*

The Church does not have the *insight*[31] or ultimate authority to establish a world leader[32], however,

---

[31] *...the Lord does not see as man sees... the Lord sees the heart.* (I Samuel 16:7).
[32] Daniel 2:20-21

we do have the authority that Christ delegated to us …authority over all the power of darkness[33] … authority over *the spirit of Jeroboam that is dividing our nation.* When the repentant[34], the uncompromisingly righteous… those who choose to identify *not as* Republicans or Democrats *but as the righteousness of God in Christ Jesus.* When they stand up and pray, they can take authority over the evil that profits from sowing *division through hostility* in our nation. They can bind that strong man in the name of Jesus and command that spirit to leave our shores and the face of the earth.

And when they have done that, *when the Church has lived up to its* **obligation to restrain evil**, then they can ask the Father in faith *to raise up godly leaders in pursuit of His righteousness and Kingdom. Leaders who will glorify Him in their*

---

[33] Luke 10:19
[34] Matthew 17:20

victories and in their service to the nations and the world.

Come Lord Jesus... Amen!

*The heartfelt and persistent **prayer of a righteous man** (believer) is able to accomplish much [when put into **action** and made effective by God—**it is dynamic and can have tremendous power**].*

(James 5:16 AMP)

The End

It has been such an honor and pleasure to serve the Lord with this Word. To bring *His light* to those of you who are willing to receive it. Those willing to work to *preserve the unity* of the church and our nation through *the bond of peace*. May God bless you and capture you with *The Truth* that is able to save you and set you free. *Amen!*

Keep the Faith!

L. C. Brown Bush

About the Author

L. C. Brown Bush is an author, a bible teacher, and a Matthew 13:52 scribe. Discipled by the Kingdom of God, her greatest joy is bringing old and new treasured revelations out of the Word of God for the enjoyment and edification of the saints.

Made in the USA
Middletown, DE
08 June 2021